NERVE CHORUS

Nerve Chorus

WILLA CARROLL

THE WORD WORKS
WASHINGTON, D.C.

Address inquiries to:
The Word Works
P.O. Box 42164
Washington, D.C. 20015
editor@wordworksbooks.org

Cover art: Chris Arabadjis
Cover design: Susan Pearce

LCCN: 2018931397
ISBN: 978-1-944585-24-2

ACKNOWLEDGMENTS

Many thanks to the editors of the following journals, who first published earlier versions of these poems:

AGNI: "Chorus of Excisions" & "Requiem for a Millennium"
CONSEQUENCE: "Falling from the Roof of the Free World"
Free State Review: "Velvet #58" & "Boomtown"
Green Mountains Review: "Mesothelioma" & "Coda"
Los Angeles Review of Books Quarterly Journal: "Broken Koan #9"
Narrative: "No Final Curtain," "They Hold Nothing Together,"
        "Memorabiliac," "Soft Resonance," "Erratica," &
        "No Apples, No Carrots, No Hay, No Grass..."
Poemeleon: "Chorus of Triggers" & "Contaminated Document"
Rogue Agent: "Choriambush"
Stone Canoe: "Matriarchive"
Structo: "Appeal"
The Equalizer: "No Eyes, No Ears, No Nose, No Tongue..."
The Rumpus: "Mammal vs. Reptile," "Juveniliac," & "Dear Tormentor"
The Tishman Review: "Green Room," "Occupational Hazards," &
        "Lamentation Street"
Tin House: "Emergency Room"
Tuesday; An Art Project: "Patrimonium," "Role of Girl As Tree," &
        "Role of Girl As Wolf"
Tupelo Quarterly: "Chorus of Omissions"
White Wall Review: "Alter Ego in Past Lives," "Nijinsky's Leap,"
        & "Broken Koan #13"
5 AM: "Back to New York" & "Dodge & Burn, Boston Navy Yard, 1967"

"Chorus of Omissions" was selected by Brenda Hillman as the
        winner of the *Tupelo Quarterly* Poetry Prize (TQ7).
"No Final Curtain" won *Narrative*'s Third Annual Poetry Contest.
Video readings of "No Final Curtain," "Memorabiliac," "Soft
        Resonance," "They Hold Nothing Together," "Yoga with
        Monica Lewinsky," & "No Apples, No Carrots, No Hay,
        No Grass..." appear in *Narrative Outloud*.
Video renderings of "Role of Girl As Wolf" & "Role of Girl As Tree"
        appear in *Tuesday; A Reading Project*.

Gratitude to my teachers and friends: Brenda Shaughnessy, Tracy K. Smith, Tina Chang, and Estha Weiner. Thank you to my Bennington Writing Seminars teachers: Major Jackson, Timothy Liu, Mark Wunderlich, and Ed Ochester. Gratitude to my Bennington undergraduate teachers: Steven Cramer and Anne Winters.

Thank you to the editors, Wyn Cooper and April Ossmann. Thanks to Joan Houlihan, Jeff Shotts, and my Colrain Conference cohort. And a standing ovation goes to Nancy White and The Word Works.

Gratitude to Judith Stonehill, Alexandra Stonehill, Mia Ting, Leila Ortiz, Stefanie Lipsey, Reyna Clancy, Heather Dobbins, Caitlin Mackenzie, Becca J. R. Lachman, Jamie Dickson, Didi Jackson, the entire Bennington Writing Seminars tribe, and my Poetry Group in NYC.

Thanks to my hometown favorites in Rochester, NY: Writers & Books, Jenny Kellogg, Albert Abonado, and Sejal Shah. Thanks to SOTA and Shari Brown. And thanks to Marcy Gamzon for sharing my work with your incredible students.

Endless gratitude to my family, especially my husband, Andreas von Scheele.

for my father,
Stephen Joseph Carroll
(1945-2015)

CONTENTS

I

II

III

IV

NO FINAL CURTAIN

The spotlight is a mean sun,
burns your paper doll,
your Icarus trick.

Your jumps are numbered.
Better to be a bird
without altitude.

Or to get out of the game early,
before they call you a gimp
with a scrapbook, or a paper crane

made by your mother's hands.
Dancing is what a flag does
with the wind.

CHORUS OF OMISSIONS

Zero my origins of industrial winter,
              my mugshot of smoke.
Zero our factories, Kodak gone bankrupt.
Omit gloved hands in glinting chemical vats,
              minus equations & patents.
Erase your pixelated face, mouth of wet vowels.
Cut the asbestos from my father's work clothes,
              minus this dust from his lungs.
Erase chalk outlines, K-9s, riots, & memory lines in my
              rust-belt revival city,
              heat-packing city,
              suffragette city,
              abolitionist city.
Erase tracks of the Underground Railroad at 25 Main
              where Frederick Douglass inked
              The North Star.
Cut cuffs from a radical in black taffeta,
              our Susan B. Anthony arrested at the ballot.
Cut skin / state / cotton / lace.
Cut the water after the bread
              & sugar skulls for the dead.
Zero the serial killer who lived at Hotel Cadillac,
              moved near our old school,
              delivered girls to the river.
Cut throat / slip tongue / wring neck / skin teeth.
Cut new glass for the voids
              in my father's jacked Ford.
Omit us, protest kids in the concrete forest, chanting:
              No Blood for Oil!
Cut our school sentry named Flash,
              a scar across his throat,
              rasping his commands at the door
              with walkie-talkie in one hand,
              my brother in the other.

Cut class under overpass.
Cut my cracker-jack-ass.
Erase purchase of dime-bag at the Drive-Thru.
Omit the jingle, *I'd rather be in Rochester, It's got it!*
Refrain my ex, of the high IQ, from doing junk at breakfast,
        overloading his blood,
        going cold at noon.
Omit twilight inside a blue glass jar,
        minus a confetti of stars,
        zero the moon Xeroxed on a pond,
        undulant ghost on dark water.
Cut film to shreds, zero the Kodachrome,
        insert megapixels & code like bright seeds.
Omit this pilgrimage back to my old room,
        minus shrines of memorabilia,
        minus all pre-digital selves.
Refrain from recollecting your lips, our collisions in bed,
        tiny gongs in my nerves,
        tidal waves of apples.
Zero the refrain, minus the song.

CHORIAMBUSH

Chorus in scrubs, come inform us—

Conduct diagnosis,
        bring us noise of prognosis,
scanning a father's lungs
        confettied with asbestos.

        Come, gloved chorus, assist us—

Deploy poison medicine
        to ventriloquist cells
signaling wild, droning refrains:
        mitosis, mitosis.

        Come to us, stricken chorus—

Open a secret room
        inside the song,
red velvet walls
        plush & nerveless.

EMERGENCY ROOM

I'm going to inspect the injury.
He removes my homemade tourniquet, a pink scarf
wrapped around a washcloth. So bright in here,
the doctors robed up, scrubbed down,
heroes in gloves.

First I'll irrigate the wound.
Fields of corn in late August, rows of green
alternating with rows of dirt. Water from the hose
tasted like green rubber & metal spigot.
We sang in school choir about Sam Patch,
who jumped Niagara falls, only to be swallowed
in the gray froth of the lesser Genesee.
The crowd stood round & held its breath,
As Sam plunged downward to his death,
O Sammy, O what a fate
for Sammy.

Now I'll apply the disinfectant.
A picnic blanket left behind in the moonlight,
like a shed wedding dress.
This clearing, flanked with trees, spiked with goldenrod,
is where you ask, *Will you?* I lie, saying, *Yes.*
Overhead the stars go slow, taking their time to arrive.
The insects move fast underneath me, assessing my body.
They have so many names, & we have so little time
to get acquainted.

I'm injecting the first shot of anesthesia.
Pain is perfect. Total. One-pointed. No maybes.
The doctor is skilled, but *you,* your touch is wrong,
always has been, your hands articulate as bread loaves,
knocking my glasses as you bumble through the motion
of stroking my hair.

It's almost over, this is the last shot.
Winter has come, the first snowfall half kills everything.
I'm numb as cotton, kissing a rubber mouth, swimming
inside a Ziploc bag.

I'm now tying the sutures.
Such delicate work. The red gash is disappearing
like a girl folding her legs,
or velvet curtains closing on a stage.
My mother is a great seamstress. I refuse
to even do buttons.

Last knot.
A scar is a seal on an inner glowing.
We grew tomatoes in the front yard. Left too long
on the vine, they would split open from their own ripeness.
I'd pick these first, before their juices expired,
opening them where they'd opened themselves. Sprinkling salt,
eating fat slices with my hands, the flesh still warm
from the sun.

ROLE OF GIRL AS WOLF

My house   torn envelope   of seeds

scorched   to speed the green   When flesh

gets audacious   nobody guards   my apertures

ports of entry   Wolves storm   a pink door

governed by holes   cracks in boards

wind slips through   gorgeous voids   Incisors

chew through wires   I put on   a pelt

of appetite   All the wrong   will flower

MATRIARCHIVE

My mother is best kept sideways.
My mother fits inside a baby tooth.
My mother is mountain.
She levitates the Pentagon in 1967.
       Wakes up the White House at 6AM, chanting:
        Hey, Hey, LBJ! How many babies have you burned today!
My mother makes masks out of clay, feathers, & twine,
       swallows antique bone buttons,
       rents an unfurnished dollhouse,
       hides under a horsehair wig.
She's a nude figure model, a hot dog stand manager,
       a census worker, a gunslinger in pirouette, a single *mater*.
She buys our sneakers at Star Market Grocery,
       hocks the piano, gives away the cat.
Her dead ex-boyfriend smelled like bourbon & pine.
My mother studies modern witchcraft to learn a few tricks,
       grows rhubarb & lemon balm,
       hides her gray with Nice 'n Easy,
       the shade called *Brunette on Fire,*
       ignites a Merit Ultra Light,
       can't hear my knock on the smoke screen.
She quit years ago, the boomerang now blooms in her chest.
Her heart is molasses in a burlap sack.
Her lungs are used envelopes, torn & burned with the old letters.

DODGE & BURN, BOSTON NAVY YARD, 1967

Stripped down with boys lined up like cattle,
my father wanted the pink slip.
His rake-thin friend fasted until too skinny
for war. Another sucked down a pack of Pall Malls
while running laps around the building—
walked in wheezing, checked every allergy on the list.
My father sat *zazen* all night, legs folded
in half-lotus, dropped acid for breakfast,
wanted a wild edge to his protest, his performance.
Faked a fail on the psychological test—
yes he had anxiety, hallucinations, night sweats,
yes he was homosexual, no he didn't like to sleep in tents,
yes he was a drug addict, yes he heard voices—
loud as the army doctor's, *Young man,*
you have some serious problems.

OCCUPATIONAL HAZARDS

Down into the bowels of a church,
feeling heat far before the boiler
room, we watch our father wrangle
a busted furnace, pipes & gaskets
fleshed with asbestos. His wrench-
grip releases microscopic fibers
flurrying the subterranean air,
lacerating his lungs, embedding
latent as radium. Bent in that storm,
we leave him, face glistening. Upstairs
we roam the body of the building,
hiding & seeking in a maze of pews,
climbing the steeple to touch
cold bells, snow on our tongues.

MAMMAL VS. REPTILE

Throws his cat into the lake,
calls her a wet rat. Gifts my mother,
his lover, a shiner. Lends me squirrel hair

paintbrushes & a postcard of Gorky's
The Liver Is the Cock's Comb, praising
pictorial language. Tackles me to dirt

& moose shit in Algonquin
by the shore, pinning my wrists
while I kick like a horse.

Son of a Buffalo steel mill worker,
builds a castle for wild mice, slips me
capfuls of peppermint schnapps,

paints his living room purple.
Praises his cat's namesake—
Isadora Duncan, radical & barefoot

mother of modern dance,
strangled by her long silk scarf
caught in the wheel of an old Bugatti.

His Isadora begs on hind legs,
leaves snakes as presents—
headless, thrashing by the door.

VELVET #58

Outside World of Inquiry #58,
KFC holds up a treeless corner, sirens
whoop. A yellowing human skeleton

presides over our library, ancient
under fluorescents, as Corey dares
me to touch jigsaw toe bones. Elbow

to elbow on choir risers, we stretch
vowels, "Follow the Drinking Gourd."
Our flanked desks make a ship

on a river flowing north to Polaris,
past industrial streets, corners patrolled
by G-Boys & Legion of Doom.

Fast forward to Corey, twenty days
from turning twenty, slipping
out the backdoor of Club Volcano,

entering an alley & a volley of fire.
Heard his folks tried to reach him
by psychic, conjuring, among others,

my name. I once stroked the blue
velvet lining his clarinet case, threads
crushed where the instrument rested.

GREEN ROOM

Before I'm born, they tend a plot
in a city yard studded with tall corn,
silk tassels rustling the night wind.
Dreams he's an insect, swaying on stalks,
sucking yellow milk beads. She pulls
the curtains of her body around me.
I'm in the green room, painting it black.
He sweeps fake snow from the set,
glinting flakes of toxic chrysotile.
I cameo as the garden—chemical revolt,
insouciant flesh, loud flower, leaf blight.
His headlights like twin moons
flood through the weeds.

II

JUVENILIAC

Retrograde through voids / cherry the score / I'm Lolita in
a Honda / obliging my elder / feeding me orange sherbet /
with his menthol fingers / Blondie on the radio / sings in
solidarity / "I Didn't Have the Nerve to Say No" / as my
tricky mentor / charmer of my mother / unzips / pulls my
head to his lap / enters the dark / theater of my mouth /
while behind the dials / a tiny Bowie struts / howling
vowels / riding diamond dogs / blowing fog / through the
speaker's holes / filling the car / parked in a broad / daylight

ROLE OF GIRL AS TREE

I go without protest   with boy

after boy   & a man   more than one

Daphne without the chase   in for something rough

bark   green sap   blond pulp   of an inner ring

I listen   to far sounds   cold surge   of water

over rocks   My father is not a river god

he cannot assist   The shape-shifting   is my own trick

further numbing transfigures   The tree becomes

a stack of two-by-fours   I can't feel a thing

My father is a carpenter   hands callused

from hammer & saw   He can't protect me

from them   He's far   across town   at the lumberyard

sawdust   like blond confetti   on his arms

PATRIMONIUM

My father is none of the above.
My father is King Lear in a pickup truck.
My father is a 2 by 4, a bronzed baby boot, a 5-cent rebate.
My father hires new children, eats blue cotton candy, wears speed skates,
       drives a green Ford Pinto with holes in the floor,
       should have been a communist.
My father is a boob man.
My father sports a headband.
My father's Personal reads: vegetarian seeks younger wife…
He's the winged monkeys of Oz.
He's a carpenter, born on Christmas, 1945.
He's a pile of sawdust, a pomegranate peddler in hell, a ticket stub.
My father is a dope pusher who gives back to the community.
My father is busted.
My father gets lost, his face on the milk,
       doesn't screen my boyfriends,
       tosses his begging bowl in the river,
       gets stuck in a huge vagina & it's not his mother's.
My father is not Darth Vader.
He's a sudden change in cabin pressure, a deer at the salt lick,
       a raven & a writing desk.
He still owes child support from previous lifetimes,
       is in the bath & can't answer your call right now…
       Does Not Go Gentle Into That Good Night,
       is not my problem after this poem.
My father claps his boy hands.
My father is dandelion, contagious.

CONTAMINATED DOCUMENT

You want a hunk of my flank? You'll swallow yellow #5, tinder, maxed-out credit cards, wet-cut hay, gunpowder, old stamps, pink clouds of fiberglass flecked with asbestos. The mind is built on wind, the more important you feel, the worse the storm. I wear my name like a tag on borrowed air. I won't administer as your night-nurse, not even in your inoculation dream. All the warm human milk in this world won't balm your need.

DEAR TORMENTOR

Epistle detonates
its body, cries no
fire in the theater.
Deploys smoke machines,
decoy trees, decades of fog.
Why did I apologize
for your skinny missive,
shoved in my mouth?
Spotlight, please—
on your cock of the walk,
your slippery zipper.
Epistle demands
you wait backstage,
dressed in shreds
of fireproof curtains,
sucking your brandy,
purpled with age,
while I flick the match,
my Dear Mentor.

ALTER EGO IN PAST LIVES

Hammers the anvil to sparks,
                conducts a chorus of crows.
Protests with turntable hands like Terminator X,
                    schooled in scratch & break.
Wants to be Joey Ramone or Thurston Moore
           on your bedroom floor.
Struts like Terspsichore in sneakers, quits ballet, studies *duende*,
                jumps like Pearl Primus,
                    stomps like Rumpelstiltskin.
Wails Fado songs in Lisbon's candlelit rooms,
           saudade croon.
Steals marble in Naples, carved body of Polyhymnia,
                stone cold, busted.
Debuts in Threepenny Opera, by & for beggars,
                    strums "Lady Stardust" in bed.
Chants the *Heart Sutra* in utero, delivers us
                from the rivers of our mothers.
Studies war no more, climbs cyclone
                  fences, unfurls soft whips,
                comes to blows & grips.

SYNAPTIC

Haywire mess of us, volted
meat, yellow fire in axon trees,

blasted branches of the vagus
nerve, wandering from brain

to gut, shunting ions, charged
when our warm tongues meet—

terpsichorean muscles, talking
straight from neuron's hot seat.

ERRATICA

No more ring around the hussy,
       pocket full of posers.
I will keep sending you a dozen
       dead horses
until you accept my steepest
       pathologies. I want to be rapt
around your linger, not Thumbelina
       under your dumb, heady for traction,
bushing around the beat. Mine own
       slash & churn, my all night
wrong, rolling in the fray,
       in the tar & weathers.

BOOMTOWN

We drank July away at Dicky's,
"Black Hole Sun" stuck on the juke.
By August, your face in my thighs,
pixelating my body with hot data.
Felt you in my skin hours after,
as sound hides in instruments at rest,
as fuel glints wet in the waiting engine
of the rocket. Noon, hard-hat men
lined up for meat in our old boomtown
as I slung hotdogs outside Kodak,
stacked cold pop, made quick change,
unlike the company towering behind me,
cranking out celluloid film, stalling
the digital, resisting the pixel, slowly
shrinking from behemoth to bankrupt
scrapper selling patents to Apple.
Here in my hands again, snapshots
of us so young, holding each other
glossy on Kodak Royal Paper.

NO APPLES, NO CLOVER, NO HAY,
NO GRASS, NO CARROTS, NO MAIZE,
NO ALFALFA, NO LINSEED,
NO DEEP BAG OF OATS

Just sugar cubes & a crop
for you. Salt licks to smart the tongue. And a long,

long lead, braided from some other
woman's hair.

APPEAL

All string, no strummer—
all static, no dial. Minus your juice,

I go slack, purpling with rain,
brain unhinged from tongue.

Amplify this body, your situation
room. Loose vector, hijacker of synapse,

come blow holes in vowels,
bum-rush the voice-box—

show face, break strike,
take back the mother-loaded, mother-

fucking night. Unzero me, lend glint,
crank nervous circuits, recruit

seventy-two muscles of voice—
wired neuronal fire.

III

CHORUS OF EXCISIONS

Cut the drill, viscous leak.
Cut salt from earth, lead from water,
        drones from firmament.
[Insert this kiss, our natural habitat]
Cut asbestos from imploding
        buildings, ban it from the wind.
Delete half-lives / Hazmat suits / atomic tourism.
Erase phosphorous clouds,
        cut nerve agents.
Cut duct tape & anaphora of ammo
        from gooseflesh.
[Insert your touch, soft impact]
[Insert rush of pearled seed]
Cut stuff with strychnine & speed.
Cut short the cutting speech.
Undercut bunk facts / crass theatrics.
Excise us, bodies up for gropes,
        strapped in the pink,
        dodging the grabs.
Strike down that crooked flag,
        deep slur on the wind.
Shred caution tape to ribbons.
Cut cluster munitions & billowing
        green chlorine gas.
[Insert your Lazarus comeback]
Cut to the chase & chastened,
        bloodhound / Technicolor face.
Cut scene to celluloid reams
        on the cutting room floor.
[Insert longing, my lifelong occupation]
Snip the roses, lacquered in Mavrik™
        pesticide blitz.
Censor the shot from *Time*
        of a charred face
        in an armored truck.

Split bitter pill, crush to smithereens.
Delete barricades for the fleeing,
      cut no holes in their hulls.
[Insert refuge, sanctuary in your scent]
[Insert flesh memory]
Extract bit rot, data decay.
Cut coal debris & PCBs from waterways—
      rewind glacial rift.
Shred empire / strike gilded set
      with my father's hammer.

FALLING FROM THE ROOF
OF THE FREE WORLD

Miscalculates the top rung,
slips, limbs flung out,
air parting for his body
called back to earth—
ankles shattering on impact,
shock muting the nerves.
Spangled in dirt & roof grit,
feet dangling at a strange angle,
my father crawls on his belly
to call for help. Before sirens,
drags himself across wet grass
for his hammer—could not stand
tools stolen or ruined in the rain
that November morning after
W's wartime reelection, fatigued
from waiting up for crushing
results & smug pundits.
From the gurney, he half-
jokes, *America broke my legs*.

EMPIRE OF STATE

Green pods split open like fat envelopes
            issuing milkweed.
Perched on telephone poles, gunshot detectors
            like sentries of percussion.
Glass beads from a firebombed car
            pelt our window.
Zip cuffs, orange jumpsuits, interrogation blitz,
            Stop & Frisk, bomb squad robots.
All night lights of the Domino Sugar Factory
            pixelate the East River,
Shreds of plastic bags garlanding our fence
            looped with razor wire.
Glaciers cut rivers through shale,
            water tastes of Xerox & rust.
Flags twist in chemical wind,
            threats level to yellow.
Striped bodies of drowned bees
            revolve in the wine press,
Venom laces the ferment, stains the tongue.

BACK TO NEW YORK

Back to all night traffic, grit-pocked snow, police choppers gyrating
river to river,
streets bobbing with human insects, fat avenues popping
with lights lights lights lights lights.

Back to billboards, four giant, long-haired Beatles, flanked by a
bitten black apple icon, floating like a Beatle heart
shucked from its body—John shot crosstown from here. "Oh Yoko!"

Back to backyards of razor wire like helixing vines, back to stray
dogs barking wildly
on caged rooftops above animal shelters.
Back to water tower skylines, pigeons circling over her majesty
the Queensboro Bridge,
exquisite loneliness of a New York Monday night.

Back to the Roosevelt Island Tram, skimming on its cable
past my window—robe undone, I wave at commuters.
Don't let them tear down the Roosevelt Island Smallpox Hospital!
Those darkening Gothic ruins are worth the ride,

highwired over the East River's lie—in truth, it's only a tidal strait,
an arm of the ocean, a leg of the sea.
Back to gliding over the oil glinted limb, imagining a sudden
plummet—velocity of free fall.

YOGA WITH MONICA LEWINSKY

I'm pretty strong for a fat girl,
she insists, wrangling a red bandana

around her hair, as if ready for a ride
in a convertible. I look into her tense eyes,

blue as a swimming pool after a drowning.
I see her face superimposed with a chorus

of TV faces, overlay of flickering masks.
I confess stealing another look at her,

supine on the mat with eyes half-closed,
irises rolled back like a doll or a trance,

whites quivering like cue balls in spin.
The tenderness I felt for her in that hour,

& whatever pleasure was hers, I will betray
at cocktail parties when I've nothing else to say.

MORE FAMOUS THAN ANDY WARHOL

Crowned Miss Sweden in '61,
my mother-in-law won fame
with a shaving cream commercial.
In black & white, her platinum locks
tickle naked shoulders, bare
except for a pearl necklace.
Take it off, take it all off—
with Noxzema!

New York party-hopping in '67,
she held court with Andy Warhol,
It was no big deal meeting Andy Warhol,
I was a bigger star than Andy Warhol.

Off-camera she smoked endless
Virginia Slims, ordered Absolut
for lunch, *Straight up in a pint glass!*
Don't bother bringing water,
I don't drink water because
fish fuck in it.

Warhol's face in *Time*, hers in *Life*.
Warhol shot, meat of his heart massaged,
saved. Her postcard from a prison inmate,
Send me a Polaroid of you wearing
nothing but red pumps.

NIJINSKY'S LEAP

Nerves are flesh violins / ballet trees / I refuse to dance
for aristocrats / My lust is Russian / mad like an eye in the
brain / Nerves are trained / electric, lunatic in moonlight /
My hand dances solo / jolts command my limbs / my skull
bones mock me / my hair is moving, for I feel it / My child
fears me / Zurich's nerve specialist / can't cure / the world
of war / I'm burning, down on all fours / When young /
my graduation / unnerved me / to feel free / to be let out /
Enervated in the asylum / after insulin shock treatments /
I can't inhabit / the air / hanging like a comma / before
landing / I barely / leave earth

RIVER ZERO

Empty vodka bottle in the freezer,
O of the metal barrel imprinting
his own temple. Not his hunting rifle,
no, a borrowed Colt. His thirst?
Can't imagine he bothered with a glass.
Last thing to touch his lips—
cold O at the mouth of the bottle,
frosted body of the bottle in hand,
tilted obliquely, above the bottle's
neck, then bottom's up, the glass O
still pressed to my uncle's lips,
though his river zero, spent.

CHORUS OF TRIGGERS

Firing a gun is no accident / She remembers his mouth / can taste it / distant peppermint // Friendly fire / blast force / radio body tally // Droning car radio / he shuts it off / kisses her hard / No accident they end up in the backseat / She names the kisses / wet pocket / bobbing apple / firecracker // Accidental misfire during gun maintenance / Or close range fire / Or metal barrel in mouth / lips wet as a kiss // Warm drones / cold reports / forces on show / fractures in the chorus

NO DRONE, NO FIRE, NO TREMOR, NO QUAKE, NO STORM, NO FLOOD, NO HEAT, NO DROUGHT, NO SIREN, NO SCENE

Only our bodies riding a bed
on a river, halfway to the rising

sea, flesh holding
back disaster.

IV

MESOTHELIOMA

Sounds like a species of coral,
or a flute carved from animal bone.
Not lesions on my father's left lung,
sheath of hard plaque tumors,
flesh trophies from his labors.
Fixed boiler pipes rife with asbestos,
installed tiles of this fireproof mineral
in housing projects now crumbling.
Worked decades as a one-man show
with a truck of tools & a flimsy mask
barely filtering drywall & joint compound
shot through with tremolite filaments.
Millimeter fibers latticed his lungs,
amassed cells in crazed refrain,
rinds of sharp grit binding his breath.
Dust clouds followed him home.
I costumed myself in his work clothes.

IN SITU

Incise the skin, crack open the ribcage.
Peel back the right lung like a curtain,
draw the other open, making a theater
of the body, heart convulsing in place.
If nerves to the brain were cut, cardiac
cells would beat onward in a slow chorus.
My brother, a trauma surgeon, pumps
a heart with his gloved hands, a heart
belonging to a construction worker
wheeled on a gurney after a massive
crane collapse. My brother's arms
tire as he feels it stop & start, stop &
start, feeling with his hands the man's
heart not wanting to stop, until it does.

BROKEN KOAN #13

after Muju & Wile E. Coyote

Unzips from head to toe / pokes holes in the hulls of boats /
shreds totem poles to walking sticks / violins to toothpicks
/ hardiest of weeds / cancers back at torn root / kisses a
duct-taped mouth / drops a cinder block from four stories
/ blowtorches glaciers / survives killing spills / spiked
boomerangs / loaded drones / nuclear fallout in the milk

LAMENTATION STREET

See my father on all fours
in the dirt like a dog
searching for curds fallen
from the moon's broken plate.
See him panting on the lawn,
lungs weedy with tumors.
Little mongrel, tethered all
evening to the porch's sagging
proscenium, taste his breath
laced with industrial debris.
Little dog, swallow your cries
until night slips its costume,
or my father his body.

BROKEN KOAN #9

after Dogen & Mumon

My face a tragic fractal mask / before the birth of my parents /
an original omen / slapped by old gods / a sky-written
emoticon / self-effacing / self-erasing / apocalyptic grin /
singing contralto through a red curtain / a nervous cameo /
caught by encores / a neuron hotel / a top animal / host to
microbes / expensive shelter / my neutrinos lost / my dark
matter abandoned / inside myself / guest inside guest

NO EYES, NO EARS, NO NOSE,
NO TONGUE, NO COLOR, NO SOUND,
NO SCENT, NO TASTE, NO TOUCH

Until theirs. I split
from nothing

into two pixels,
deep in their bodies.

SOFT RESONANCE

after Josef Albers's Homage to The Square

Childhood rattles in a box of lemonheads
from Marv's Deli, sour at first suck, color of lost teeth.
Nobody ever bought Marv's pickles from the huge jar
by the register, the brine more green than yellow,
piss of a jilted lover. Marv's burned to the ground.
Jaundice & alarm. Satin & caution. Please, a glass
of milk. Peel the stretched eggshell membrane,
licked with a German sadness. As with people,
so with color, except the dying.

REQUIEM FOR A MILLENNIUM

What are these spirits that inhabit
our bodies trying to tell us?
            —Kazuo Ohno, Butoh dancer

Ghost clown in drag,
skin greased white, sheds
his mother's kimono,

swims sinuous limbs
in glacial striptease,
mouth a red river,

nonagenarian hands
conducting isotopes,
body a spectral

tango, a shivering
amphibian, blown
towards footlights

of the millennium,
as he throws roses
back into the ocean of us.

THEY HOLD NOTHING TOGETHER

My mother reigns as queen of buttons.
Her prized ones: brass, copper, wood,
abalone, mother-of-pearl, celluloid
bonded with toxins. She tests one
with her teeth to see if ivory or plastic.
Puncture by hot needle sorts out fakes
from real tortoiseshell, buffed like glass.
Her favorites are the big ones, two inches
tall. *Some are worth money, so when I die,
don't just give them away.* Scattered
around her they shine a jigsaw sea.
History in the palm of your hand.

MEMORABILIAC

I was once a gap-toothed woman, a finger-
                sucking kid, a locked-up case, a cut peach,
      a flag in the wind,
           a weed in the sidewalk crack.
I was hungry until Mom's paycheck,
           broken into by the neighbor boys,
      camped out in the phone booth,
                half-orphaned until my father called.
I was once a rider of mastodons,
           a waitress showing skin,
                a footprint filled to the brim.
I was hustler / hoe / Emerson / Thoreau,
           player of pin the tail on the honky,
      a dead man limping,
           siren wail / siren tail,
              cilia slung,
        flagellum propelled,
        almost mammal.
I was once incognito in bed,
           rust in the wound, mirror in the spoon,
      fruit too rotten to name,
           mistress of the survival game.
I once heard he still appled my core,
           pocketed a torch,
        kept the photographs in a box under the porch.

CODA

The first tumor distends
through his shirt like a cartoon
heart beating out of its chest—
others wrangling liver & spleen.
We are carrion & meteor, our meat
dressed in fire & diaphanous gas.
How to measure dark matter
amidst bright coordinates of stars?
At the cusp, as breath constricts,
slows—we betroth to zero,
held in a dilating spotlight.

NOTES

"Choriambush": The title embeds the word "choriambus," a metrical verse-foot of two unstressed syllables between two stressed ones, derived from the Greek *khoreios*, meaning "of the dance."

"Mammal vs. Reptile": The painting by Arshile Gorky, "The Liver Is the Cock's Comb" (1944), is in the collection of the Albright-Knox Art Gallery in Buffalo, NY.

"Velvet #58": In the spiritual, "Follow the Drinking Gourd," the drinking gourd is code for the Big Dipper. The song has played a part in the Civil Rights Movement, folksong revival, and educating elementary school students about the Underground Railroad.

"Patrimonium" adapts a line from Lewis Carroll and another from Dylan Thomas.

"Alter Ego in Past Lives" names the song, "Lady Stardust" by David Bowie, and adapts lyrics from the spiritual, "Down by the Riverside."

"Boomtown" names the song, "Black Hole Sun" by Soundgarden. The poem refers to the invention of the first digital camera in 1975 by Kodak engineer Steve Sasson; company executives resisted the technology, viewing it as a threat to film.

"Chorus of Excisions" refers to Kenneth Jarecke's photograph of an Iraqi man burned alive in the Gulf War. I'm indebted to Torie Rose Deghett's "The War Photo No One Would Publish," TheAtlantic.com (Aug. 8, 2014).

"Nijinsky's Leap" draws from *The Diary of Vaslav Nijinsky*, ed. by Joan Acocella, and Frank Bidart's "The War of Vaslav Nijinsky."

"Soft Resonance" takes its title from a painting by Josef Albers, "Homage to Square: Soft Resonance" (1962), in the collection of the Memorial Art Gallery, Rochester, NY.

"No Eyes, No Ears, No Nose, No Tongue...": The title is borrowed from the text of the *Prajñaparamita*, a Mahayana Buddhist Sutra also known as the *Heart Sutra*.

ABOUT THE AUTHOR

Willa Carroll's poems have appeared in *AGNI, Los Angeles Review of Books Quarterly Journal, Tin House*, and elsewhere. A finalist for The Georgia Poetry Prize, she was the winner of *Narrative*'s Third Annual Poetry Contest, as well as *Tupelo Quarterly*'s TQ7 Poetry Prize, judged by Brenda Hillman. Video readings of her poems were featured in *Narrative Outloud* and *Tuesday; A Reading Project*. Carroll holds an MFA from Bennington Writing Seminars and has taught at universities, writing centers, and public schools. A former experimental dancer and actor, she has collaborated with performers, multimedia artists, and her filmmaker husband on text-based projects. She lives in New York City. Visit her website, www.willacarroll.com.

ABOUT THE ARTIST

Chris Arabadjis is a visual artist based in New York City. His work has been shown in Manhattan, Brooklyn, Boston, San Francisco, and Iowa City. His work can be seen in the Pierogi Flat Files, and he was a SciArt Center featured artist in 2017. Arabadjis' work was included in the July 2017 issue of Physics Today, International Author's *Emanations* anthologies edited by Carter Kaplan, and *Devouring the Green: Fear of a Human Planet: An Anthology of New Writing*, edited by Sam Witt. He received an MFA from Pratt Institute and studied Theoretical Nuclear Physics at UMass Amherst. He is interested in simple systems, cellular automata, loose algorithms, and degrees of unpredictability. Visit his website, www.chrisarabadjis.com.

ABOUT THE WORD WORKS

Since its founding in 1974, The Word Works has steadily published volumes of contemporary poetry and presented public programs. Its imprints include The Washington Prize, The Tenth Gate Prize, The Hilary Tham Capital Collection, and International Editions.

Monthly, The Word Works offers free literary programs in the Chevy Chase, MD, Café Muse series, and each summer it holds free poetry programs in Washington, D.C.'s Rock Creek Park. Word Works programs have included "In the Shadow of the Capitol," a symposium and archival project on the African American intellectual community in segregated Washington, D.C.; the Gunston Arts Center Poetry Series; the Poet Editor panel discussions at The Writer's Center; Master Class workshops; and a writing retreat in Tuscany, Italy.

As a 501(c)3 organization, The Word Works has received awards from the National Endowment for the Arts, the National Endowment for the Humanities, the D.C. Commission on the Arts & Humanities, the Witter Bynner Foundation, Poets & Writers, The Writer's Center, Bell Atlantic, the David G. Taft Foundation, and others, including many generous private patrons.

An archive of artistic and administrative materials in the Washington Writing Archive housed in the George Washington University Gelman Library. It is a member of the Community of Literary Magazines and Presses and its books are distributed by Small Press Distribution.

wordworksbooks.org

OTHER WORD WORKS BOOKS

Annik Adey-Babinski, *Okay Cool No Smoking Love Pony*
Karren L. Alenier, *Wandering on the Outside*
Karren L. Alenier, ed., *Whose Woods These Are*
Karren L. Alenier & Miles David Moore, eds.,
       Winners: A Retrospective of the Washington Prize
Christopher Bursk, ed., *Cool Fire*
Willa Carroll, *Nerve Chorus*
Grace Cavalieri, *Creature Comforts*
Abby Chew, *A Bear Approaches from the Sky*
Barbara Goldberg, *Berta Broadfoot and Pepin the Short*
Akua Lezli Hope, *Them Gone*
Frannie Lindsay, *If Mercy*
Elaine Maggarrell, *The Madness of Chefs*
Marilyn McCabe, *Glass Factory*
Kevin McLellan, *Ornitheology*
JoAnne McFarland, *Identifying the Body*
Leslie McGrath, *Feminists Are Passing from Our Lives*
Ann Pelletier, *Letter That Never*
Ayaz Pirani, *Happy You Are Here*
W.T. Pfefferle, *My Coolest Shirt*
Jacklyn Potter, Dwaine Rieves, Gary Stein, eds.,
       Cabin Fever: Poets at Joaquin Miller's Cabin
Robert Sargent, *Aspects of a Southern Story*
       & A Woman from Memphis
Miles Waggener, *Superstition Freeway*
Fritz Ward, *Tsunami Diorama*
Amber West, *Hen & God*
Nancy White, ed., *Word for Word*

THE WASHINGTON PRIZE

Nathalie Anderson, *Following Fred Astaire*, 1998

Michael Atkinson, *One Hundred Children Waiting for a Train*, 2001

Molly Bashaw, *The Whole Field Still Moving Inside It*, 2013

Carrie Bennett, *biography of water*, 2004

Peter Blair, *Last Heat*, 1999

John Bradley, *Love-in-Idleness: The Poetry of Roberto Zingarello*, 1995, 2ND edition 2014

Christopher Bursk, *The Way Water Rubs Stone*, 1988

Richard Carr, *Ace*, 2008

Jamison Crabtree, *Rel[AM]ent*, 2014

Jessica Cuello, *Hunt*, 2016

Barbara Duffey, *Simple Machines*, 2015

B. K. Fischer, *St. Rage's Vault*, 2012

Linda Lee Harper, *Toward Desire*, 1995

Ann Rae Jonas, *A Diamond Is Hard But Not Tough*, 1997

Susan Lewis, *Zoom*, 2017

Frannie Lindsay, *Mayweed*, 2009

Richard Lyons, *Fleur Carnivore*, 2005

Elaine Magarrell, *Blameless Lives*, 1991

Fred Marchant, *Tipping Point*, 1993, 2ND edition 2013

Ron Mohring, *Survivable World*, 2003

Barbara Moore, *Farewell to the Body*, 1990

Brad Richard, *Motion Studies*, 2010

Jay Rogoff, *The Cutoff*, 1994

Prartho Sereno, *Call from Paris*, 2007, 2ND edition 2013

Enid Shomer, *Stalking the Florida Panther*, 1987

John Surowiecki, *The Hat City After Men Stopped Wearing Hats*, 2006

Miles Waggener, *Phoenix Suites*, 2002

Charlotte Warren, *Gandhi's Lap*, 2000

Mike White, *How to Make a Bird with Two Hands*, 2011

Nancy White, *Sun, Moon, Salt*, 1992, 2ND edition 2010

George Young, *Spinoza's Mouse*, 1996

THE HILARY THAM CAPITAL COLLECTION

Nathalie Anderson, *Stain*
Mel Belin, *Flesh That Was Chrysalis*
Carrie Bennett, *The Land Is a Painted Thing*
Doris Brody, *Judging the Distance*
Sarah Browning, *Whiskey in the Garden of Eden*
Grace Cavalieri, *Pinecrest Rest Haven*
Cheryl Clarke, *By My Precise Haircut*
Christopher Conlon, *Gilbert and Garbo in Love*
         & *Mary Falls: Requiem for Mrs. Surratt*
Donna Denizé, *Broken like Job*
W. Perry Epes, *Nothing Happened*
David Eye, *Seed*
Bernadette Geyer, *The Scabbard of Her Throat*
Barbara G. S. Hagerty, *Twinzilla*
James Hopkins, *Eight Pale Women*
Donald Illich, *Chance Bodies*
Brandon Johnson, *Love's Skin*
Thomas March, *Aftermath*
Marilyn McCabe, *Perpetual Motion*
Judith McCombs, *The Habit of Fire*
James McEwen, *Snake Country*
Miles David Moore, *The Bears of Paris*
         & *Rollercoaster*
Kathi Morrison-Taylor, *By the Nest*
Tera Vale Ragan, *Reading the Ground*
Michael Shaffner, *The Good Opinion of Squirrels*
Maria Terrone, *The Bodies We Were Loaned*
Hilary Tham, *Bad Names for Women*
         & *Counting*
Barbara Ungar, *Charlotte Brontë, You Ruined My Life*
         & *Immortal Medusa*
Jonathan Vaile, *Blue Cowboy*
Rosemary Winslow, *Green Bodies*
Michele Wolf, *Immersion*
Joe Zealberg, *Covalence*

INTERNATIONAL EDITIONS BOOKS

Kajal Ahmad (Alana Marie Levinson-LaBrosse, Mewan Nahro
    Said Sofi, and Darya Abdul-Karim Ali Najin, trans., with
    Barbara Goldberg), *Handful of Salt*
Keyne Cheshire (trans.), *Murder at Jagged Rock: A Tragedy by Sophocles*
Jeannette L. Clariond (Curtis Bauer, trans.), *Image of Absence*
Jean Cocteau (Mary-Sherman Willis, trans.), *Grace Notes*
    Yoko Danno & James C. Hopkins, *The Blue Door*
Moshe Dor, Barbara Goldberg, Giora Leshem, eds., *The Stones
    Remember: Native Israeli Poets*
Moshe Dor (Barbara Goldberg, trans.), *Scorched by the Sun*
Lee Sang (Myong-Hee Kim, trans.), *Crow's Eye View: The Infamy of Lee
    Sang, Korean Poet*
Vladimir Levchev (Henry Taylor, trans.), *Black Book of the
    Endangered Species*

THE TENTH GATE PRIZE

Jennifer Barber, *Works on Paper*, 2015
Lisa Lewis, *Taxonomy of the Missing*, 2017
Roger Sedarat, *Haji As Puppet*, 2016
Lisa Sewell, *Impossible Object*, 2014

CPSIA information can be obtained
at www.ICGtesting.com
Printed in the USA
FSHW01n1059161018
52957FS